Parents' notes

This fun-filled activity dictionary has so much to keep children amused while they are learning.

Each double page has a beautifully illustrated picture packed full of items beginning with a letter of the alphabet. There is a wealth of detail for readers of all ages to pore over.

Each page also has a puzzle activity, a joke and some silhouettes to identify.

The dictionary entries each have their own little picture and an accompanying phrase or rhyme. These have been devised to cater for children's fascination with the sound that words make.

Children will enjoy getting their tongues round the humorous verses and this playing with rhyme is the perfect preparation for becoming a reader.

Younger children will enjoy finding the ten listed items in amongst the busy large picture.

Older children (and adults!) might like to search to find the many extra items that begin with each particular letter. You will find a checklist of the illustrated items at the back of the book.

This book can be dipped into and enjoyed on many occasions and in many ways. It offers an early introduction to alphabet order and a delightful means of expanding a child's vocabulary.

a b c d e f g h i j k l m n o p q r s t u v w x y z

Angry ants, adorable aunts
Angular anchors aweigh
Active acrobats, acorns and apples
Alligators (all A).

acorn
An acre of acorns

ant
A line of angry ants

acrobat
An active acrobat

antelope
The antelope ran up the slope.

alligator
An agitated alligator

apple
A juicy apple

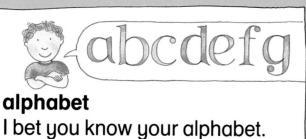

alphabet
I bet you know your alphabet.

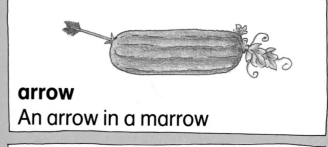

arrow
An arrow in a marrow

anchor
The heavy anchor sank her.

astronaut
An astronaut out for a walk.

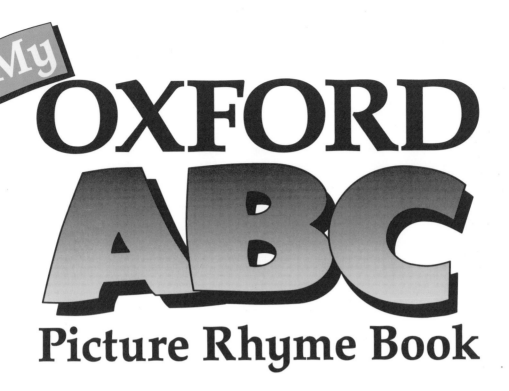

My OXFORD ABC

Picture Rhyme Book

With rhymes by
Roger McGough

Compiled by
Dee Reid

Illustrated by
Debi Gliori

Oxford University Press

Oxford University Press, Great Clarendon Street, Oxford OX2 6DP

Oxford   New York
Athens   Auckland   Bangkok   Bogotá   Bombay
Buenos Aires   Calcutta   Cape Town   Dar es Salaam
Delhi   Florence   Hong Kong   Istanbul   Karachi
Kuala Lumpur   Madras   Madrid   Melbourne
Mexico City   Nairobi   Paris   Singapore
Taipei   Tokyo   Toronto

and associated companies in
Berlin   Ibadan

Oxford is a trade mark of Oxford University Press

© Oxford Unviersity Press 1990, 1991, 1994
© Word Rhymes: Roger McGough 1990
© Text: Dee Reid 1990

First published as *The Oxford ABC Picture Dictionary* 1990
Redesigned edition 1994
5 7 9 10 8 6 4

Enquiries concerning reproduction outside these terms and in other countries
should be sent to the Rights Department, Oxford University Press, at the address
above.

ISBN 0 19 910328 3 (paperback)

A CIP catalogue record for this book is available from the British Library

Printed in Hong Kong

Aa

See you later alligator.

In a while crocodile.

Use the stepping stones to hop along the alphabet path.

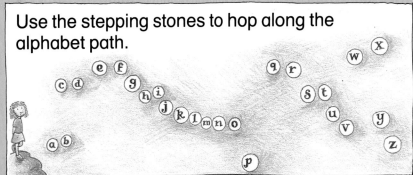

Say 'Hello' to Bill Buffalo
On his bicycle there.
Best balancer in the business
Better than any bear.

baby
A bouncing baby

bicycle
Can you ride a bicycle?

badger
Don't badger a badger.

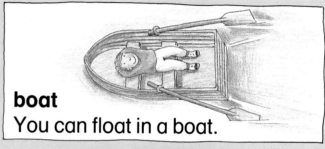

boat
You can float in a boat.

balloon
The balloon popped.

bulldozer
A bulldog in a bulldozer

bear
A hairy bear

bus
A double-decker bus

bee
Buzzing bees

butterfly
A butterfly fluttered by.

Bb

What do you call a sleeping bull?

A bulldozer.

Use the **b** in the balloon to make some words.

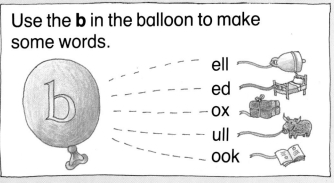

- ell
- ed
- ox
- ull
- ook

a b c d e f g h i j k l m n o p q r s t u v w x y z

Take a bow, cow. Why?
Without you cornflakes would be too dry
Coffee and cocoa undrinkable
Imagine a world without moo-cows? Unthinkable.

camel
A camel with a camera

clock
An alarm clock

camera
A video camera

clown
A clumsy clown

car
A racing car

computer
A computer keyboard

castle
A spooky castle

cow
How now brown cow?

caterpillar
A caterpillar with a catapult

crab
A crab might grab you.

Cc

How do you count cows?

With a cowculator.

Find homes for these things that begin with **c**:

cat
cow
canary
car
caterpillar

Two identical dentists sharing a surgery
One called Dennis, the other Sammy
Dennis likes his doughnuts sugary
Sammy, jammy.

daffodil
Daffodils grew on the hills.

dolphin
A diving dolphin

dentist
Two identical dentists

donkey
'Hee-haw,' says the donkey.

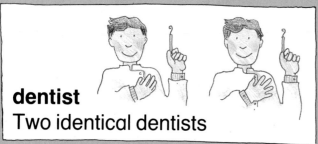

dinosaur
Diplodocus (dip-*plod*-o-kuss)

dragon
A fire-breathing dragon

dog
Does a dog yap in your lap?

drum
Beat the drum.

doll
A doll in a doll's pram

duck
'Quack, quack, come back,'
said mother duck.

Dd

When is it time to see the dentist?

2.30

Can you match the rhyming pairs?

dog   big
dice   lock
door   mice
dock   log
dig   floor

a b c d e f g h i j k l m n o p q r s t u v w x y z

They are building an escalator
Up Mount Everest they say
So that mountaineers like us
Can conquer it each day.

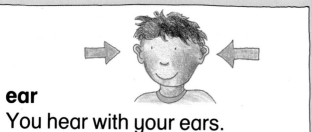

eagle
An eagle in its eyrie

engine
A car engine

ear
You hear with your ears.

envelope
A letter in an envelope

eel
As slippery as an eel

escalator
An alligator on an escalator

egg
Would you expect
an egg to explode?

exit
An extra exit

elephant
Eleven elephants

eye
I saw his eye was sore.

Ee 11

Why do elephants have trunks?

They'd look funny with suitcases, wouldn't they?

A ewe is a mother sheep. Find babies for each of these mothers:

cow   duck   cat   frog

a b c d e f g h i j k l m n o p q r s t u v w x y z

Do you know where factories come from?
They are manufactured intact
Made in Factory factories
As a matter of fact.

factory
A toy factory

flowers
A bunch of flowers

feather
A bird wears its feathers
in all weathers.

fox
The fox slept in its hole.

fire engine
The fire engine's siren wailed.

frog
A freckled frog on a lily leaf.

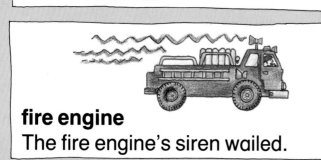

fish
Wish for a fish on your dish.

fruit
Some fruit in a boot

flag
Would you wag a flag
or let it sag?

frying pan
Six sizzling sausages
in a frying pan

Ff

What do frogs drink?

Croaka Cola.

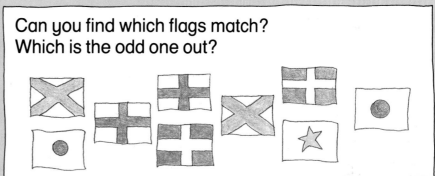

Can you find which flags match?
Which is the odd one out?

a b c d e f g h i j k l m n o p q r s t u v w x y z

Guy the gorilla played guitar
And wanted to be a superstar
So he formed a group with a goat and a gnu
You can hear them nightly at the zoo.

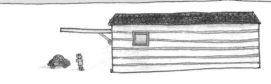

garage
A large garage.

goat
A goat in a boat.

gate
A squeaky gate.

goldfish
Three goldfish in a bowl.

giraffe
A giraffe in the bath.

gorilla
A gorilla at the tiller.

gloves
A pair of gloves.

grass
The green grass grows.

glue
Gummy glue will stick to you.

guitar
An electric guitar

Amina —
find a
helicopter
balloon
aeroplane
kite

Why are goldfish orange?

Because the water makes them rusty.

Tell the story of The Gingerbread Boy

1.
2.
3.
4.
5.
6.

Here comes a hamster with a hammer
Hide the nail
The last time he played handyman
He hurt his tail.

hammer
A hammer and nails

helmet
A fireman's helmet

hamster
A hamster in a cage

hippopotamus
A happy hippo

harp
A carp playing the harp

house
A house for a mouse

hedgehog
A tickly, prickly hedgehog

hovercraft
The hovercraft
laughed at the raft.

helicopter
A rescue helicopter

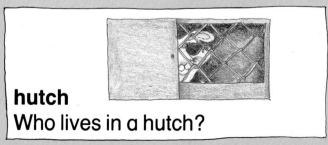

hutch
Who lives in a hutch?

Hh

What do you get when you cross a giraffe with a hedgehog?

An 11 metre hairbrush.

Humpty Dumpty sat on a 🧱 had a great fall.
All the King's 🐴🐴🐴
and all the King's 👮👮👮
Couldn't put 🥚 together again.

a b c d e f g h i j k l m n o p q r s t u v w x y z

There is an inkstain on the iceberg
Which means someone has been there
Writing inspiring verses
A poetic polar bear ?

ice
It's nice to see mice on the ice.

iguana
An iguana eating a banana

iceberg
I spy an iceberg.

ink
A bottle of ink

ice cream
Chocolate ice cream

insect
I expect you can
inspect an insect.

icicle
I see an icicle on my tricycle.

island
I land on an island.

igloo
Can you glue an igloo?

ivy
I've an ivy on my wall.

Ii

Knock, knock.

Who's there?

Felix.

Felix who?

Felix my ice cream, I'll lick his.

Insects have six legs. Match the things with the number of legs they have.

2   3   4   6   8   100s

a b c d e f g h i j k l m n o p q r s t u v w x y z

A juggler from Jarrow called Klug
Could juggle with a chinaware jug,
Cheap jewellery, jam jars and jigsaws,
Orange jelly and a Japanese mug.

jacket
A leather jacket

jigsaw
Jim saw a jigsaw.

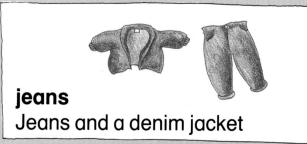

jeans
Jeans and a denim jacket

jockey
A jockey playing hockey

jellyfish
A jellyfish on a smelly dish

judge
A jolly jumping judge

jet
Get a jet to Japan.

jug
A jug and a mug on a rug

jewellery
A jewellery box

juggler
Can a juggler juggle with a jug?

Jj

What jam can't you put on your bread?

A traffic jam.

Here is a jigsaw puzzle. Fit the pieces together to make some farmyard friends.

a b c d e f g h i j k l m n o p q r s t u v w x y z

The kangaroo is the king of karate
(His belt is black)
Kicking quarrelsome kids at a party
(They'll not come back.)

kangaroo
The kangaroo has lost his shoe.

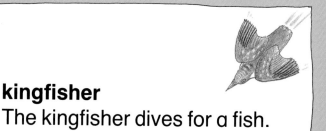

kingfisher
The kingfisher dives for a fish.

kennel
Who sleeps in this kennel?

kitten
Can you count the kittens?

key
He kept the key in the ketchup.

knife
Who knows where a knight
keeps his knife?

kilt
He spilt his milk on his kilt.

knitting
The kitten was sitting
on the knitting.

king
The king wore a ring.

koala
Carla kept a koala in the parlour.

Kk

What's this?

A koala climbing up a tree.

Help the kangaroo to jump along the number path.

 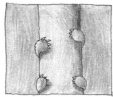

Can you do it backwards?

a b c d e f g h i j k l m n o p q r s t u v w x y z

'What is wrong with the rungs on a ladder,'
Said the lady with a leaden frown,
'Is that although there are lots for climbing
There are too few for coming down.'

ladder
An adder had a ladder.

leopard
A leopard who is hiding.

lake
Can you bake a cake on a lake?

lifeboat
Launch the lifeboat.

lamb
A lamb on wobbly legs

lighthouse
A lighthouse on a hill

leaves
In autumn the leaves
leave the trees.

lion
I wouldn't lie on a lion.

lemonade
A litre of lemonade

lollipop
A lollipop in a shop

LI

Why couldn't the leopard escape from the zoo?

Because he was always spotted.

Which one has the most spots?

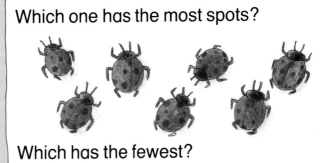

Which has the fewest?

Monkeying around in a garage
A monkey one midsummer day
Tinkered with a motorbike engine
Which roared and took him away.

magician
A magnificent magician

mirror
See your reflection in the mirror.

magpie
A magpie stole a magnet.

mole
A mole in a mole hole

map
A treasure map

monkey
A cheeky monkey

menu
When you choose from the
menu, choose for me and you.

mouse
One mouse in a house.
Two mice eating rice.

milk
A milk shake

motorbike
I'd like a motorbike.

Mm

What do mice do in the daytime?

Mousework.

What words can the magician make with his magic m?

m op
an
at
ix
ud

a b c d e f g h i j k l m n o p q r s t u v w x y z

Nettles sting if you fall on them
(It's their way of saying 'How do you do?')
Better ring if you call on them
And only shake hands with your shoe.

nail
Don't fail to hit the nail.

nettle
A stinging nettle

neck
Is your knee next to your neck?

newspaper
A daily newspaper

necklace
A gold necklace

nightingale
A nightingale sings at night.

needle
Do you need a needle?

nurse
A nurse lost her purse.

nest
A bird has a rest in its nest.

nut
A squirrel cracking nuts

Nn 9 ♩♪

What's the difference between a nail and an unlucky boxer?

One's knocked in and the other's knocked out.

Which bird belongs to which nest?

eagle

house martin

blackbird

penguin

a b c d e f g h i j k l m n o p q r s t u v w x y z

A lot of otters wearing overalls
As hot as oven gloves
Trot off down to the river
Which is what an otter loves.

oak
An oak tree is taller than me.

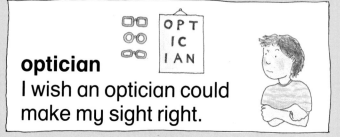

optician
I wish an optician could make my sight right.

oar
Paddle with a paddle or an oar.

orange
An orange is orange but this melon is lemon.

oats
Goats eat oats.

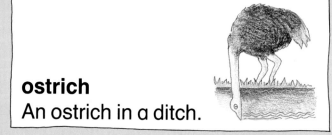

ostrich
An ostrich in a ditch.

ocean
Does the motion of the ocean make you ill?

otter
The otter has a lotta fun!

oil
I'll oil the engine.

owl
How'll the owl use a towel?

Oo

What do you get if you cross an owl with a skunk?

A bird that smells but doesn't give a hoot.

Can you make all these words from the letters on the octopus' legs?

red	bed	bear
ear	cat	rat
bat	dot	rot

How many more can you make?

a b c d e f g h i j k l m n o p q r s t u v w x y z

Hiccup, Hiccup, Hiccup,
Goes the prickly porcupine
Supine after a super supper
Of pickles, pork pies and port wine.

panda
A panda and a gander

pelican
An American pelican

parachute
A parakeet in a parachute

pencil
Draw around a stencil
with a pencil.

parrot
The parrot pecked a carrot.

pineapple
A piece of pickled pineapple.

peach
Have a peach each.

pirate
Would you fire at a pirate?

peacock
As proud as a peacock

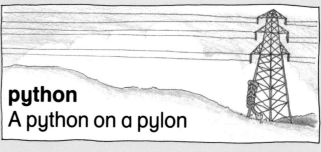

python
A python on a pylon

Pp

What do porcupines eat with cheese?

Prickled onions.

Can you copy like a parrot? Point to the matching words.

Goodbye
Hello
Pretty boy
Got any food?
Let me out

Got any food?
Hello
Goodbye
Pretty boy
Let me out

a b c d e f g h i j k l m n o p q r s t u v w x y z

Hey diddle diddle, here is a riddle
To puzzle out if you can.
What is found in a river (and ends in shiver)
Ring o'roses, red noses and Gran?

queen
The queen quickly
asked a question.

rake
Can you make
a cake with a rake?

queue
A queue for the boat

rhinoceros
A rhinoceros seems big to us.

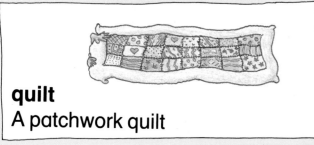

quilt
A patchwork quilt

robin
A robin bobbing up and down

rabbit
A rabbit is nibbling a radish.

robot
Robert the robot

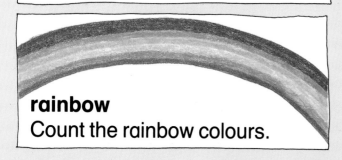

rainbow
Count the rainbow colours.

roller boots
Roll along on roller boots.

Qq Rr

What did the robot say to the petrol pump?

Take your finger out of your ear when I'm talking to you.

The baby rabbit has got lost in his burrow. Which tunnel leads to his mother?

a b c d e f g h i j k l m n o p q r s t u v w x y z

Don't go sliding on the ice in your slippers
It's so slippery that certainly you'll slip
Put on a penguin suit and flippers
To be sure that you get the perfect grip.

sand-castle
A sand-castle at the seaside

skateboard
A skunk on a skateboard

sausage
A sausage in a saucepan

snail
A snail's silvery trail

scarecrow
A tattered and torn scarecrow

spider
I spied a spider.

seagull
Can you see a seagull?

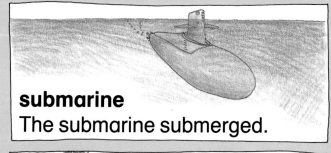

submarine
The submarine submerged.

sheep
Seven shaggy sheep
should be shorn.

swing
Will a king sing on a swing?

Ss

Can you find ten seaside things hidden in
the seaweed?

a b c d e f g h i j k l m n o p q r s t u v w x y z

Don't put two teapots together
They will tittle ~ tattle like mad
About tea things like teabags and teaspoons
And the wonderful teatimes they had.

tee~hee

taxi
Elephants need a maxi taxi.

toad
A toad crossing the road

teddy bear
The teddy bear has lost its hair.

tractor
He backed the tractor up the hill.

telephone
A teeny-tiny tortoise
is on the telephone.

train
The train came and went again.

television
Cartoons on the television

tree
Can you see the bee in the tree?

tent
A bent tent

tricycle
You could try a tricycle if you
fall off a bicycle.

Tt

What's yellow and white and travels at over 100 mph?

A train driver's egg sandwich.

Use the typewriter to type these words:

tap   tin   ten   top   tug   tea

Q W E R T Y U I O P
A S D F G H J K L
Z X C V B N M

a b c d e f g h i j k l m n o p q r s t u v w x y z

While a vulture plays the violin
To a vicar on a verandah
A unicorn blows its horn
And dances with a panda.

umbrella
Tell her to sell her umbrella.

vet
I bet a vet could get a pet.

unicorn
A unicorn has a magic horn.

video
Cartoons on video

uniform
A uniform can keep you warm.

violin
What a din from the violin.

vase
A vase of various violets

volcano
A vole on a volcano

vegetable
A vegetable on the table

vulture
A vulture and a viper on a van

Uu Vv

What goes up when the rain comes down?

An umbrella.

A vet helps sick animals. What jobs do these people do?

a b c d e f g h i j k l m n o p q r s t u v w x y z

How much wood does it take to make a woodpecker?

How many walnuts are there in a wall?

Can a winkle wink? A wombat bat?

Does wearing wellies make you well? (That's all!)

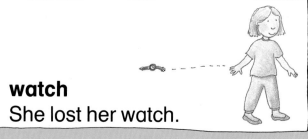

watch
She lost her watch.

windmill
A windmill on a hill

water
The porter brought the water for his daughter.

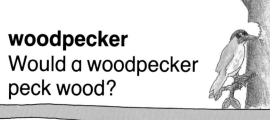

wood
Would wood taste good?

wheel
We'll wheel the wheel to the wall.

woodpecker
Would a woodpecker peck wood?

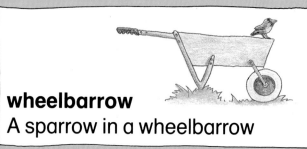

wheelbarrow
A sparrow in a wheelbarrow

wool
We wound some white wool.

whistle
Can you whistle on a thistle?

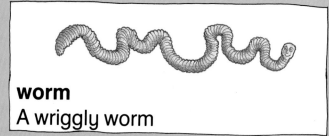

worm
A wriggly worm

Ww

How do worms fall over?

With great difficulty.

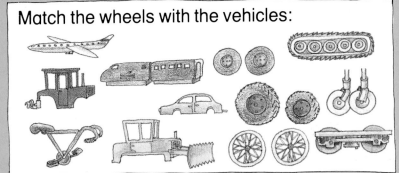

Match the wheels with the vehicles:

a b c d e f g h i j k l m n o p q r s t u v w x y z

'Yuk!' says the yak, 'it tastes like spam,
Mother's home-made yellow yam jam.'
An ox exclaimed, 'Please give me a pot
The zebras at the zoo will soon scoff the lot.'

X-ray
He examined the
X-ray excitedly.

yoghurt
Yoghurt is yummy.

xylophone
A xylophone makes
a ringing tone.

yo-yo
Have a go-go on my yo-yo.

yacht
Have you got a yacht?

zebra
Debra the zebra

yak
A yak in a mac

zero
Three, two, one, zero

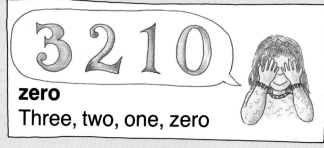

yellow
The yellow yolk of an egg

zoo
See a gnu at the zoo.

Xx Yy Zz

What is yellow and very dangerous?

Shark infested custard.

Match the footprints with the correct colour.

yellow
red
blue
green
orange

Did you find all these objects in the big pictures?

A
abacus
ace
adder
admiral
aerial
aeroplane
albatross
alien
ambulance
angler
antimacassar
antlers
ape
apricot
aquaduct
aqualung
aquarium
arch
archery
arm
armadillo
artichoke
artist
awning
axe

B
baby
basket
bat
beard
bell
binoculars
blanket
bluebell
bone
book
boomerang
bottle
box
boy
bread
bridge
bulrush
burrow
butter

C
cable
cactus
cage
cake
calculator
calendar
canary
cape
cards
casters
catapult
cauliflower
chain
chair
chandelier
chess
chicken
children
chimpanzee
claw
clogs
cloud

cobweb
cockerel
coffee jug
cogs
colander
comb
confetti
conjuror
cormorant
cot
crane
crate
crocodile
crocus
crow
cuckoo clock
cucumber
cuff
cup
curlers
curtains

D
daffodil
dartboard
darts
deckchair
delicatessen
designer
dice
d.i.y.
doctor
dominoes
double bass
doughnut
dove
drain
draughts
drawing board
drill
drink
dungarees

E
ear-ring
earth
eclair
Egyptian
electric bulb
elf
elk
elm
Ely
embroidery
emerald
emu
entrance
engineer
equator
Evesham
Exmouth
express
extinguisher

F
face
fan
farm
February
fence
ferret

ferry
film
finger
finger-print
fir
fireman
fireworks
fish fingers
five
flame
flamingo
flask
flats
flour
flowers
football
forget-me-not
fork
forklift truck
fountain
French windows
Friday
fruit
funnel

G
gas
gasket
geranium
gerbil
gherkin
ghost
giant
gingerbread man
glasses
glider
gnu
goggles
golf
gooseberry jam
grapefruit
grease
green paint
greenhouse
grill
guide
gum

H
hacksaw
hair
hairbrush
hair-dryer
hamburger
hand
handbag
handcuffs
handkerchief
hare
harmonica
high chair
hive
honey
hoof
hook
horn
horseshoe
hose
house
hyacinth

I
ice cubes
ice skates
illustrator
infant
instrument
ironing board

J
jackal
jackdaw
jack-in-a-box
jam tarts
jelly babies
jelly beans
jester
jet
jewellery
jogger
joke book
judo
juice
juke box
jump

K
kid
kilt
kiss
kitchen
knapsack
knee
knickers
knob
knot

L
label
lace
laces
ladle
lamp
lantern
leap-frog
lemonade
lens
letter
lettuce
library
life-jacket
lightning
lilies
log
look-out
lorry
luggage

M
macaw
mackintosh
magazine
magnifying glass
magnolia
maid
mail-box
maize
man
mandarin
mandolin
marbles
marigold
marmalade
Martian

mashed potato
mask
mast
match
mattress
measles
medal
medicine
melon
meringue
microscope
money
moose
moth
mouse-trap
moustache
muesli
multiplication
mushroom
mussels

N
narcissus
nasturtium
net
netball
nib
nine
North
November
nozzle
nutmeg

O
oboe
observatory
omelette
orbit
organ
origami
outboard motor
oven
oyster

P
pail
paint
paintbrush
palette
palm tree
pansy
panther
parasol
patchwork
path
pear
pen
penny farthing
perch
periscope
photo
picnic basket
pie
pillow
plait
polar bear
pony-tail
poodle
porcupine
postman
potty

puddle
puffin
Punch and Judy
puppet
pushchair
pyramid

Q
quintuplets

R
raincoat
rattle
recorder
Red Riding Hood
reindeer
reins
rhubarb
ribbon
rock
rocket
rope
rose bush
roundabout
rubbish bin
rucksack
ruler

S
sailboat
sailor
sand
sandals
sandwich
scarf
scooter
screw
screwdriver
sea anemone
sea urchin
seal
seaweed
shark
shell
shoes
shorts
shower
sign
sketchbook
sky
snorkel
snowman
socks
spades
spanner
squirrel
starfish
stick
stork
strawberries
string
sun
sun-hat
sun-umbrella
surfboard
swan
swimmer
swimsuit

T
table
tambourine
tangerine

tapes
tea
teacup
tea-tray
tennis ball
tennis racket
thesaurus
thimble
thread
tie
tiger
tights
tinsel
toadstool
toast
toboggan
tomato
tongs
toothpaste
torch
track
trout
trunk
turkey
typewriter

U
vanilla ice-cream

V
vest
video camera
viewing gallery
vine

W
waistcoat
waitress
walrus
wallpaper
wand
wardrobe
washing
washing line
waterfall
watering can
waterlily
wave
weasel
web
wedding
wellington boots
Wendy House
wheelchair
whiskers
wicker basket
wings
wizard
wolf
woman
woollen jumper
woolly hat

X
yawn

Y
yoga
Zeno

Z
zeppelin
zip
Zodiac
zoom
zzzz

How many more can you find?